BASICS OF STOCK MARKET

S. S. Kadganchi

PREFACE

"An investment in knowledge pays the best interest."
– Benjamin Franklin

Investment in stock market has witnessed unprecedented growth worldwide especially in the last two decades. Growth in stock market has been parallel to the growth of economy. Investing in stock market requires requisite skills and adequate understanding of market dynamics and tools of investment.

With that intention this book is to not only provide a direction towards investments for beginners, but also aims to offer fresh ideas for experienced investors to educate while making an investment in financial market.

The purpose of this book is to provide adequate information so that all type of investors, common people, students can acquire and gain new skills and expand their knowledge, in order to accomplish profitable investments in the stock market!

There are a lot of people these days "playing" the stock markets. It can be fun, exhilarating and sometimes, it's almost intoxicating! But, it's not a game! Investigate your investments, define your goals and objectives, and invest your money instead of just "playing" with it!

This book mainly highlighted to create awareness among common people, saver and investors towards basic knowledge of stock market such as Guidelines to enter in financial market and stock market, how to transaction took place, ways to make share trading, basic direction of building portfolio of investors, types of various investment avenues, Analysis of Portfolio management , Portfolio management process, how investors manage portfolio& book the profit and hedge against risk by various techniques, Mutual fund and different types of Mutual fund etc.

The book comprises of six chapters. First Chapter provides basics of guidelines of Stock market which includes Importance of Stock market, types of financial markets, participants and players in stock market and pricing of shares in the stock market.

Chapter Two describe the financial transaction process in stock market, which will investors will familiar with Demat Account, Types and process to open Demat Account, require eligibility and important documents required for Demat Account process, basic guidelines about online and offline transaction in stock market and various features and characteristics of online& offline trading. Third chapter involve Stock Market Indices were investors gain knowledge about the concept of SENSEX AND CNX NIFTY. Chapter Four highlighted Financial Instruments which common investment player aware about the Basic concept of Financial services and instruments such as Shares, types& Features of Share capital, Mutual Fund-Types, features, Derivative Market-Types, participants in derivative market, Commodity Market etc.

Chapter Fifth highlights Security Analysis which is require to aware about how to build Investors portfolio and requires techniques to get make profitable investment proposal's-Such as Fundamental and Technical Analysis. Chapter Six -Portfolio Management which readers will get the direction about building their own profitable portfolio, which involves- types of portfolio, role of portfolio manager, process of portfolio management and practical example of Portfolio management.

Stock market investment can be fun and interesting but all good things come at a price. The price you have to pay here is just a bit of research into yourself, understand how much risk you can take, what kind of an investor you are, which kind of stocks are available in the market and which suits you more. Invest now and enjoy the benefits of it later!

Happy Investing!

Sufficient care has been taken while preparing the manuscript for the book. However there may be some unintentional errors. Readers are welcome to send all comments, suggestions to S. S. Kadganchi
Email ID- sskadganchi.36@gmail.com

TABLE OF CONTENT

TABLE OF FIGURES

Chapter -1

"What is Stock Market?"

1.1 Introduction:

A stock market is also known as share market it is a place where buyers and sellers of shares come together to invest their money in shares or in other securities; Share or a Stock is a small part of business which represents ownership claims on business. In return a part of a company's profit that is paid to the shareholders is known as dividend.

Stock/Share market is divided in two major parts Primary Market and Secondary Market. It provides long term and secured funds to the companies to expand their businesses. There are a number of financial assets used for market trade, including equity shares, debentures, commodity, derivatives etc. These are used by the investors to make a profit out of their respective markets. All of these are called capital market instruments because these are responsible for generating funds for companies, corporations, and sometimes national governments.

The New York Stock Exchange (NYSE) is arguably the most powerful stock exchange in the world; it was not the first exchange to exert influence on the markets.

In the 1300s, Venetian moneylenders began to sell debt issues to other lenders and to individual investors. In the 1500s, Belgium's exchange dealt exclusively in promissory notes and bonds.

In the 1600s, the emergence of various East India companies that issued stock led to a financial boom, which was followed by a bust when it was revealed some companies conducted very little actual business.

In 1611, the world's first stock exchange (in it's modern sense) was launched by the VOC in Amsterdam.

In Robert Shiller's own words, the VOC was "the first real important stock" in the history of finance. One of the oldest known stock certificates, issued by the VOC chamber of Enkhuizen, dated 9 Sep 1606.Competition from the NASDAQ (National Association of Securities Dealers Automated Quotations System), which was formed in 1971 to trade securities electronically, has caused the NYSE to evolve and innovate in order to cement it's dominance as the premier global exchange.

In India the Bombay Stock Exchange (BSE) and the National Stock Exchange (NSE). The BSE has been in existence since 1875. The NSE, on the other hand, was founded in 1992 and started trading in 1994.

1.2 Definition:

- "It is a place where Companies raise the funds from the public by issuing the securities"
  For e.g. Shares, Bonds, Debentures etc.

- "The stock market is a platform which provides the long term finance to the businesses to start the new ventures or further expansions by issuing the shares to the public."

1.3 Why it is important?

Stock market is an important part of the economy of a country. The stock market plays a vital role in the growth of the industry that affects the economy of the country. This is the only reason that the government, industries and even the central banks of the country keep a close watch on the happenings of the stock market. The stock market is important from both the industry's point of view and the investor's point of view as well.

The primary purpose of stock market is to provide funds to the companies. Wherever the companies needed funds for the further expansion or setting up a new business they have to take loans from the financial institutions or they have to issue shares through the stock market.

This is the primary function of the stock exchange and thus they play the most important role of supporting the growth of the industry. That is the reason a rising stock market is the sign of a developing industrial sector and a growing economy of the country.

There is an economic relation between the demand and supply chain and availability of money in economy.

Stock market directly impact this relation in various ways,

1. It helps in the growth of company.
2. It helps the growth of investors.
3. It helps the government to plan developmental projects for better economy.
4. It helps banks and financial institutions to earn more money.
5. It provides better saving options than the traditional ways of saving.

1.4 Different Types of Market Cap's & Sectors

The stock market is divided according to the market capitalization of the company and by sector.

Market capitalization refers to the total market value of a company's outstanding shares and it is calculated by multiplying those outstanding shares by the current market price of one share.

1. Large Cap: Large-cap companies are generally regarded as those with a market capitalization of $10 billion or more.
2. Mid Cap: mid-cap companies are those with a market capitalization of between $2 billion to $10 billion.

3. Small Cap: small-cap companies fall between $300 million to $2 billion.

1.4.1 Sectors

The stock market is divided into 11 sectors,

1. Energy
2. Materials
3. Industrials
4. Consumer Discretionary
5. Consumer Staples
6. Health Care
7. Financials
8. Information Technology
9. Telecommunication Services
10. Utilities
11. Real Estate

1.5 How it works?

As we all know how important it is to invest money in the right financial instrument. Stock market investment is a modern way for investors to earn high returns. How it works? It is essential to know about it's workings we get a rough idea about it from figure 1.0. Let's get back to the basics and learn how the stock market works in India.

How the stock market works (Figer-1)

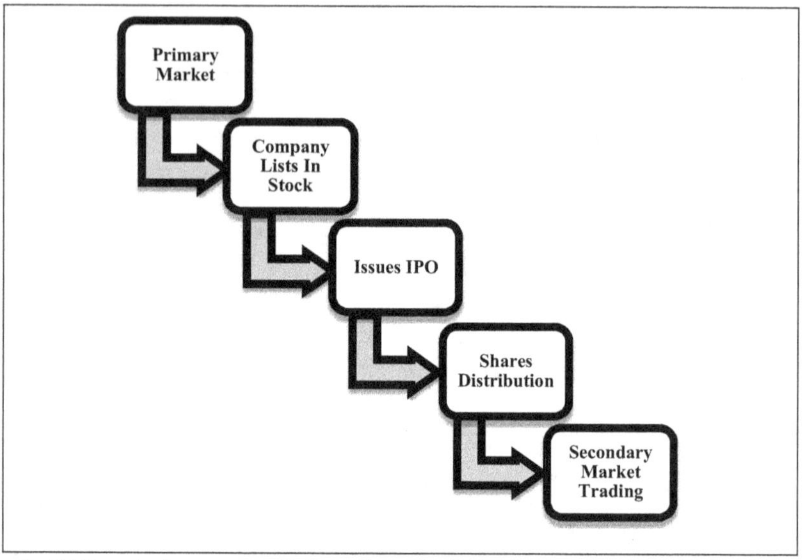

1.6 Participants of the Stock Market:

The stock market is a way where investors can invest in shares, bonds, securities and derivatives. This investment is facilitated by stock exchanges; there are some important participants who are working to make these transactions run smoothly.

1. Securities and Exchange Board of India (SEBI):

SEBI is one of the important participants of stock market. SEBI is the regulator of stock markets in India and it ensures that stock markets in India work in order. SEBI is a regulatory framework which is controlling the exchanges, companies, brokerages, and other participants to protect investors.

2. Stock exchanges:

The stock market is a way where investors invest in shares, bonds, and derivatives. This trading is facilitated by stock exchanges. In India, there are two primary stock exchanges on which companies are listed for the first time.

Bombay Stock Exchange (BSE) – Sensex is it's index

National Stock Exchange (NSE) – Nifty is it's Index

3. Stock brokers/brokerages:

Broker is an intermediary (middleman) that executes buy and sells orders for investors in return of a fee or a commission.

4. Investors and traders:

Investors who purchase stocks to become an part of ownership in the company. Trading involves buying or selling the equity in the short term period. To understand this concept in a better way we have to learn about primary and secondary markets.

1.7 Primary Markets

The primary market provides an opportunity to issuers of stocks, especially for the corporate to raise the funds they needed for the further expansions or to start a new business venture.

In the primary market companies can issue the shares through the Initial Public Offer (IPO).A company sells it's shares for the first time to the public. An IPO opens for a particular period.

Within this period investors can bid for the shares and buy them at the issue price announced by the company.

For this, companies had to pay a fee to the stock exchanges. They are also required to provide all important details of the company's financial information like quarterly/annual reports, Balance sheet etc. to the stock markets.

1.8 Secondary Market

The secondary stock market is where shares of a company are traded after being initially offered to the public in the primary market. It is a market where buyers and sellers meet directly. This buying and selling transactions work through stockbrokers/brokerage firms, who work as a middleman between investors and the stock exchange.

1.9 Pricing of Shares in the Stock Market

The only goal of a every investor to earn good returns through the stock market. For this, we have learn how to properly value a company and it's share price.

• When the demand for shares is more than supply, price rises.

• When the demand for shares is less than supply, price falls.

The Indian stock exchanges, BSE and NSE, have methods that determine the price of stocks on the basis of volume traded and these prices changes in a fraction of the seconds. So this is how the stock market works in India.

Chapter-2

"How transactions take place in Stock Market?"

2.1 What is Demat Account?

2.1.1 Features of a Demat account

2.1.2 Key elements of a Demat account:

2.2 Types of Demat account

2.3 How to open Demat account Offline?

2.3.1 Introduction

2.3.2 Steps involved in opening a Demat account (Offline Process):

2.4 How to open Demat account online?

2.4.1 Steps to open a Demat account online:

2.4.2 Eligibility of Investor

2.4.3 List of accepted KYC documents:

2.4.4 Important terms & conditions in opening Demat account

2.4.5 Different charges associated with a Demat account

2.5 What is Online Trading?

2.5.1 How to Trade Online

2.6 Intra-Day Trading

2.6.1 Intraday Trading Strategies for Beginners

2.7 T+2 Settlements

To make a transaction in stock market investor has to open a Demat account.

2.1 What is Demat Account?

A Demat account is a depository where the digital copies of your stocks can be stored and managed. In other words, a Demat Account allows investors to hold shares and securities in electronic format, with an aim of facilitating safe, easy and convenient trade for users. It is just like a bank account, the only difference being that when a bank account holds cash, the Demat account holds shares and other securities.

Online trading in the stock market will find the entire procedure of investing, trading, holding, and monitoring faster, convenient and cost-efficient with use of Demat account. It also allows the investor to buy and sell or hold a whole lot of products, other than shares and stocks, bonds, mutual funds, government securities, or exchange-traded funds. All this can be done from the comforts of your home with the click of a mouse, and without any paperwork.

According to the Securities Exchange Board of India (SEBI), a demat account is mandatory for anyone trading in financial securities.

2.1.1 Features of a Demat account

In the physical form there are chances of shares and stocks getting misplaced, damaged etc. Demat account provides this safety concern as here the securities are stored in electronic format. Other features of a Demat account are:

- **Easy Access:** Demat accounts are completely online, it can be easily accessed online from any part of the world and at any time.

- **Variety holdings:** One can hold various investments like mutual funds, equity shares, bonds and exchange-traded funds under one Demat account.

- **Quick Monitoring:** Demat accounts facilitate easy monitoring of the holdings from the comforts of one's home.

- **Saves time:** With everything in digital format, this online platform makes trading very convenient and less time-consuming. One can buy, sell or transfer funds and securities in seconds.

- **Minimal Costs:** There are no additional costs of stamp duty, handling charges, etc. involved when you are trading with a Demat account.

- **Corporate Gains:** Dividends, interest, or refunds reach the Demat account holder without any delay. Be it bonus issues, stock split or rights shares, everything is automatically updated in the Demat accounts.

- **Investment transfer:** The account holder can transfer all or part of their holdings to another person. The account holder only needs to fill a Delivery Instruction Slip with the accurate information and the seamless transfer of shares or other holdings can be carried out.

- **Dematerialization:** The investor can choose to convert their physical share certificates or other physical records of securities into electronic form through the process of dematerializing.

- **Collateral for loan:** The value of the security holdings can be used as collateral while applying for a loan.

- **Freeze the account:** Available only when you have specific securities in your demat account, this facility can be used when the investor expects any inconvenient activities to occur. You can freeze your demat account similar to how you block a bank account or a credit card.

2.1.2 Key elements of a Demat account:

- **Depository:**

There are two authorized depositories operating in India, Central Depository of Securities Ltd (CSDL) and National Depository of Securities Ltd (NSDL). These two institutions electronically hold pre-verified shares.

- **Depository Participant (DP) (Broker or Portfolio manager):**

Any financial institution that is registered under SEBI can act as an Agent of the Depository and conduct transactions for the in investor. Any depository service has to be channelled through the DP. A DP can be a financial institution, a scheduled commercial bank, a foreign bank operating in India (RBI approved), a stockbroker, a clearinghouse, a state financial corporation, a share transfer agent, a non-banking financial company, etc. SEBI assigns every DP a unique code.

- **Investor:**

The investor is the individual is the owner of the securities. In this case, the person holding the demat account is the investor.

- **Unique ID:**

Every demat account has a unique 16-digit identification number which ensures smooth and transparent processing of securities.

2.2 Types of Demat account

There are three types of demat accounts which can be opened in India, depending on the residential status of the investor:

1. **Regular Demat account:** Investors residing in India.

2. **Repatriable Demat account:** NRIs who hold a non-resident rupee account (NRE) can open this type of demat account. This account allows the international transfer of funds.
3. **Non-repatriable Demat account:** non-resident Indians with a non-resident ordinary rupee (NRO) account can open this type of demat account. However, this does not allow for international transfer of funds.

2.3 How to open Demat account Offline?

There are two modes available to open a Demat account offline and online we are going to see both of them in detail as under:

2.3.1 Introduction

The Depository Act of 1996 has made it easier for everyone to manage their financial securities in a few clicks. Instead of receiving physical copies of shares or other securities, a demat account helps you to leverage the benefits of an online trading platform where you hold your financial security on a standardized electronic system.

The Government of India introduced the provisions for a demat account in 1996 to keep up with the evolving times where most developed countries offered electronic trading platforms to reduce fraud, improve market efficiency, and ease trading.

2.3.2 Steps involved in opening a demat account (Offline Process):

Opening a demat account is easy. It can be done in two ways: offline and online. Let's take a look at how to open a Demat account offline.

- **Select a Depository Participant:**

  Once you have compared the services and benefits offered by different DPs, you can finalize the most suitable DP for your needs.

- **Fill application form:**

You will need to fill out an application form for opening a new Demat account. Along with this, you will need to submit a list of KYC documents such as Identity Proof, Address Proof, PAN card, Bank details, and your personal details.

- **Verification process:**

You will be given a list of rules and regulations to ensure ethical and legal trading, and to clear any doubts you may have regarding holding a demat account and the different functions it serves. The DP will conduct an in-person verification of you and your KYC documents. You will have to pay any necessary fee associated with opening a demat account. The fee depends on the existing policy of the DP. The fee differs from DP to DP.

- **Final approval:**

Once your documents are verified, and the final formalities are completed, your new demat account will be opened. You will also be given the Unique Identification Number for your account.

2.4 How to open Demat account online?

There is a more convenient way of opening a demat account; with the use of computer/ laptop/tab/smartphone, you can open your demat account in a few minutes.

2.4.1 Steps to open a Demat account online:

- Head to the official website of your preferred DP.
- Fill out the simple lead form asking for your name, phone number and city of residence. You will then receive an OTP on your registered mobile number.
- Enter the OTP to get to the next form. Fill in your KYC details such as date of birth, PAN card details, contact details, bank account details.
- Your demat account is now open! You will receive details such as demat account number on your email and mobile.

An investor can have multiple demat accounts.

These accounts can be with the same DP, or with different DPs. As long as the investor can provide the required KYC details for all applications, they can open multiple Demat accounts.

2.4.2 Eligibility of Investor

- Any registered resident of India with the necessary documentation to prove it can open a demat account in India. With certain restrictions under SEBI, even non-resident-Indians can open a demat account.
- A demat account can have up to three account holders; two joint account holders and one main account holder.
- Just like with bank accounts, there is a provision to nominate a nominee in case of death.
- In case of joint account holders, each account holder is encouraged to nominate a nominee. The nominee can be changed or updated as per the wishes of the account holder.

2.4.3 List of accepted KYC documents:

In order to open a demat account, you will require certain documents. You will need one proof of identity and one proof of address. Here is a list of accepted documentation that can serve as:

- Proof of identity
- Passport
- Driver's license
- Voter's ID

- IT returns
- Verified copy of electricity/phone bill
- PAN card
- A photo ID card issued by a central or state government body
- Proof of address
- Ration card
- Bank passbook/ bank statement

2.4.4 Important terms & conditions in opening Demat account

- Individual should ensure that the papers are valid as on submission date and that they haven't crossed the expiry date. Also, the personal details need to be provided in the prescribed format.
- Most of the brokers/ banks pre-fill them once you provide them with PAN number and Date of Birth. You need to verify and attest them.
- Your Bank Account number and IFSC code need to be shared for opening a Demat account.

- You will have to share with the DP two copy passport size photo, Savings bank account-cancelled cheque leaf/ bank statement /passbook with IFSC and MICR printed on it, Pan card details, Aadhar or voter id details and Income proof - bank statement of 6-month transaction (only for F&O).

2.4.5 Different charges associated with a Demat account

The fee depends on the DP and their policy. Usually, there is a one-time account opening fee; an annual maintenance fee; dematerialization fee; a transaction fee/commission on every transaction made by the DP.

2.5 What is Online Trading?

Online trading involves the trading of securities through an online platform. Online trading portals facilitate the trading of various financial instruments such as equities, mutual funds, and commodities.

2.5.1 How to Trade Online

- **Open Demat and Trading Account:**

To begin trading online you need to open an online trading account with an online broking firm. It is essential to choose a broker who is a registered member of all the stock exchanges and is certified by the SEBI.

- **Learn all the Stock Market Basics:**

The stock market functions on the system of supply and demand. Learning to trade begins with gaining more knowledge about the share market investment. Keeping tabs on financial news and websites, listening to pod-casts and taking up investing courses are all excellent ways to become an efficient investor.

- **Practice with an Online Stock Simulator:**

Online stock trading simulators are a great way to learn online trading. Since it is a simulator, the losses you make would not affect you; hence you can learn trade without any fear. There are many simulator games available on play store such as Binomo, Moneybhai.com.

- **Draft a plan:**

  While you trade, it is very important to think through your investment strategies. Decide in advance how much you are willing to invest in a particular company and set limits on the amount of loss you are willing to bear.

If you bear all these points in mind, online share trading will be an easy and profitable task for you. Practice is the key to successful online trading. Stock trading is a long-term investment and requires patience and perseverance.

It involves buying and selling of securities such as stocks, bonds, and other related financial instruments online. For this purpose, you will require a Demat account and a trading account. A Demat account acts as the common repository to store the purchased units of stocks whereas the trading account acts as the platform to buy and sell the share. A bank account is linked to the trading account to facilitate funding of trade. The major benefit of online trading is that investor can seek the help of dedicated customer care in case of any clarifications or queries.

2.6 Intra-Day Trading

Intraday trading is the practice of purchasing and selling financial securities in a single trading day. Traders involved in this practice are referred to as "day traders". This trade is especially critical to traders who are looking to make quick gains in a single trading day.

In A day trading we can get more returns as compare to other financial instrument in a short time period but there is huge risk involved in the day trading, because of that sometimes the beginners may lose their money. Before starting a intraday trading they should have a proper knowledge about the risk and return concept, Entry and Exit point from the particular security & most importantly they should have proper knowledge of technical analysis to became a successful trader.

Here are some of the basics required to be a successful day trader;

- **Sufficient Capital**

  A large amount of capital is necessary to capitalize effectively on intraday price movements. Sometimes we have purchase extra shares when the price falls and after when the price goes ups, we can make extra profits.

- **Knowledge and Experience of the Marketplace**

Individuals who attempts to day trade without an understanding of market fundamentals they lose money. Technical analysis and chart reading are both good skills for a day trader should have.

- **Strategy**

There are some different strategies day traders use including swing trading, arbitrage, short selling and trading news. These strategies are more complicated and advanced until they produce regular profits and well limited losses.

- **Discipline**

Success is impossible without discipline. A profitable strategy is useless without discipline.

2.6.1 Intraday Trading Strategies for Beginners

- **Following the trend**:

  The individual who follows the trend will buy when price goes up or short sell when the price falls. This is done on the assumption that prices that have been rising or falling increasingly will continue to do.

- **Contrarian investing**:

  This strategy assumes the rise in prices will reverse and drop. The contrarian buys during the fall or short-sells during the rise, with the express expectation that the trend will change.

- **Scalping**:

  This is a style where a speculator exploits small price gaps created by the bid-ask spread. This technique normally involves entering and exiting a position quickly within minutes or even seconds.

- **Trading the news**:

  Investors using this strategy will buy when good news is announced or short sell when there's bad news. This can lead to greater volatility, which can lead to higher profits or losses.

- **Stop-loss order:**

  A stop-loss order is an order placed with a broker to buy or sell a specific stock once the stock reaches a certain price. A stop-loss is designed to limit an investor's loss on a security position.

The most important benefit of a stop-loss order is that it costs nothing to implement. Your regular commission is charged only once the stop-loss price has been reached and the stock must be sold. One way to think of a stop-loss order is as a free insurance policy.

2.7 T+2 Settlements

In financial markets T+2 is shorthand for trade date plus two days indicating that securities transactions must be settled. The rules or customs in financial markets are for securities transactions to be settled within a commonly understood 'settlement period'.

Chapter-3

"Stock Market Indices"

3.1 Introduction

A stock market index is a statistical measure that reflects changes taking place in the market. It's calculated by grouping a few similar stocks listed on the stock exchange and the selection criteria for the calculation could be the size of a company, market capitalization or type of industry.

Stock market indexes around the world are powerful indicators for global and country-specific economies. In India there are two types of indices used by NSE and BSE.

3.2 SENSEX

Sensex stands for "sensitive index", it represents BSE (Bombay Stock Exchange). Sensex indicates all major companies of BSE. Sensex is calculated using share prices of top 30 companies which are listed in BSE. If the Sensex goes up it means that share values of most of the top companies have gone up and if it goes down it means other top companies shares also goes down.

S&P BSE SENSEX, first compiled in 1986, was calculated on a "Market Capitalization-Weighted" methodology of top 30 stocks representing large, well-established and financially sound companies across the sectors.

In September 1, 2003, S&P BSE SENSEX is being calculated on a free-float market capitalization methodology. The "free-float market capitalization-weighted" methodology is a globally followed index construction methodology; all major index providers like MSCI, FTSE, STOXX, and Dow Jones use the free-float methodology.

3.2.1 SENSEX - Stock Selection Criteria

The general guidelines for selection of constituents in SENSEX are as follows:

- **Listed History:**

The stock should have a listing history of at least 3 months on top 10 in the list of BSE.

- **Trading Frequency:**

The stock should have been traded on each and every trading day in the last three months at BSE.

- **Final Rank:**

The stock should be in the top 100 companies listed by final rank.

- **Market Capitalization Weightage:**

The Weightage of each stock in SENSEX based on three-month average free-float market capitalization should be at least 0.5% of the Index.

- **Industry/Sector Representation:**

Stock selection would generally take into account a balanced representation of the listed companies in the universe of BSE.

- **Track Record:**

In the opinion of the BSE Index Committee, the company should have an acceptable track record.

3.2.2 Free-float Methodology Concept

Free-float Methodology refers to an index construction methodology that takes into consideration only the free-float market capitalization of a company for the purpose of index calculation and assigning weight to stocks in the Index.

3.2.3 Definition of Free-float

"The shares traded on the daily basis in stock exchange are included in free-float."

Specifically, the following categories of shareholding are generally **excluded** from the definition of Free-float:

- Shares held by founders/directors which has control element
- Shares held by persons/ bodies with "Controlling Interest"
- Shares held by Government as promoter/acquirer
- Holdings through the FDI Route

- Strategic stakes by private corporate bodies/ individuals
- Equity held by associate/group companies (cross-holdings)
- Equity held by Employee Welfare Trusts
- Locked-in shares and shares which would not be sold in the open market.

The remaining shareholders fall under the Free-float category.

We can understand the Free-float methodology in a simple way from the following example;

3.2.4 Example of Free-float methodology

Company "XYZ Ltd' issues 10000 shares, out of which 2000 shares held by government, 5000 shares by directors of the company and remaining 3000 shares are available in the open market for trading. Market price of share is 100

Total Shares = 10000

Shares Held by Government = 2000

Shares Held by Directors = 5000

Shares available in the Open Market = 3000

Market price of share = 100

Here total market capitalization of the company is 10,000 × 100= 10, 00,000

Free float market capitalization of the company is 3000 × 100= 300,000

According to the rules of BSE any shares which do not fall under the above categories are considered as free float (open market) shares.

3.3 CNX NIFTY

The CNX Nifty is used in the National Stock Exchange of India Ltd. (NSE). The Index focuses on the behaviour of blue-chip companies, the largest and most liquid Indian securities. It includes top 50 companies listed on the NSE, it is calculated by float-adjusted market capitalization methodology and it shows the true reflection of the Indian stock market. The CNX Nifty is very much useful for benchmarking, index funds and index-based derivatives.

3.3.1 Stock Selection Criteria for CNX Nifty

Selection of the index set is based on the following criteria:

- **Liquidity:** The security should have traded at an average impact cost of 0.50% or less during the last six months, for 90% of the observations. Impact cost is the cost of executing a transaction in a security in proportion to it's index weight, measured by market capitalization at any point in time. This is the percentage mark-up suffered while buying/selling the desired quantity of a security compared to it's ideal price - (best buy + best sell)/2.

- **Float -Adjusted Market Capitalization:** Companies must have at least twice the float-adjusted market capitalization of the current smallest index components.

- **Float:** Companies should have at least 10% of it's stock available to investors (float). For this purpose, float is stocks which are not held by the promoters and associated entities (where identifiable) of such companies.
- **Domicile:** The company must be domiciled in India and trade on the NSE.

- **Eligible Securities:** All common shares listed on the NSE are eligible for inclusion in the CNX Nifty index. Convertible stock, bonds, warrants, rights, and preferred stock that provide a guaranteed fixed return are not eligible.

3.3.2 Price Index Calculations Formula

The CNX Nifty is computed using market capitalization weighted method wherein the level of the Index reflects the total market value of all the stocks in the Index relative to the base period November 3, 1995.

Free Float Market Capitalization =

Equity Capital * Price * IWF (Investible Weight Factors)

Index Value = Current Market Value / Base Market Capital * Base Index Value (1000)

Base market capital of the Index is the aggregate market capitalization of each stock in the Index during the base period. The market cap during the base period is equated to an Index value of 1000 known as the base Index value.

3.3.3 Investable Weight Factors (IWFS)

IWF as the term suggests a unit of floating stocks available for trading in terms of available number and which is not held by the entities having strategic interest in a company. The following categories are excluded from the free float factor:

- Shareholding of promoter and promoter group
- Government holding in the capacity of strategic investor
- Shares held by promoters through ADR/GDR
- Strategic stakes by corporate bodies
- Investments under FDI category

- Equity held by associate/group companies (cross-holdings)
- Employee Welfare Trusts
- Shares under lock-in category

3.3.4 Example of CNX NIFTY calculation

For XYZ Ltd.

	Shares	%
Total Shares	**100,00,000**	**100**

	No. Of Shares	%
Shareholding of promoter and promoter group	19,75,000	19.75
Government holding in the capacity of strategic investor	50,000	0.50
Shares held by promoters through ADR/GDRs.	2,50,000	2.50
Equity held by associate/group companies (cross-holdings)	12,575	0.13
Employee Welfare Trusts	1,45,987	1.46
Shares under lock-in category	14,78,500	14.79

IWF = [1,00,00,000 – (19,75,000 + 50,000 +2,50,000 +12,575 +1,45,987 +14,78,500)] / 1,00,00,000 =0.60870

Chapter-4

"Types of Financial Instruments"

4.1 Shares

4.1.1 Equity Shares:

4.1.2 Preference Shares:

4.1.3 Types of Preference shares:

4.2 Mutual fund:

4.2.1 Types of mutual funds:

4.3 Debentures & Bonds:

4.3.1 Types of Debentures:

4.4 Government securities:

4.5 Money Market instruments:

4.6 Derivatives:

4.6.1 Types of Derivatives:

4.6.2 Participants in the derivatives market:

4.7 Commodities:

4.7.1 Mostly preferred commodities by investors

4.1 Shares

A stock market or share market is a place where buyers and sellers of shares, Share or a Stock is a small part of business which represents ownership claims on business. Shares are also known as scrip. There are two types of Shares as follows,

4.1.1 Equity Shares:

Equity shares are also known as ordinary shares. Equity shareholders are the members of the company who are having voting rights and they are equally sharing the profit as well as the loss of a company.

❖ **Features:**

- Equity shareholders are the real owners of a company.
- Voting rights while selecting the management of a company.
- Right to attend the annual general meetings.
- No fixed rate of dividend.

4.1.2 Preference Shares:

Preference shareholders are having some preferential rights like to get the dividend and also repayment of capital at the time of winding up or liquidation of a company. They get the fixed rate of dividend.

❖ **Features:**

- Fixed rate of dividend.
- Preferential rights to get dividend and repayment of capital before equity shares.

4.1.3 Types of Preference shares:

1. **Cumulative-** In this type of preference Shares Company has to pay the dividend at any cost company either earns a profit or that doesn't matter.
2. **Non-cumulative-** These shares are treated like normal preference shares. If a company earned the profit then only, they get the dividend.
3. **Redeemable-** These shares have a right to claim for after a fixed time period the company has to pay the capital raised form these types of shareholders.
4. **Irredeemable-** Irredeemable shares are permanent in nature and the shareholdings continues till the company goes to liquidation.

5. **Participative-** These shareholders receive the fixed rate of dividend and also they have a right to participate in surplus of profit along with equity shares.
6. **Non-Participative-** Most of the preference shares are Non-Participative in nature and they don't have any right to claim for extra earnings.
7. **Convertible-** Convertible shares are those which are converted into equity shares after a specific time period.
8. **Non-Convertible-** Non-Convertible shares have no rights to convert into equity shares.

4.2 Mutual fund:

A mutual fund is an investment in which it pools the money of investors and invests in stocks, bonds, money market instruments and other types of securities. Mutual fund is an easiest way for beginners who do not understand much about investing. Investors can choose a mutual fund scheme based on their financial goal. In order to make money by investing in mutual funds, it is important to know what the types of mutual fund.

Structure of Mutual Fund (Figure-2)

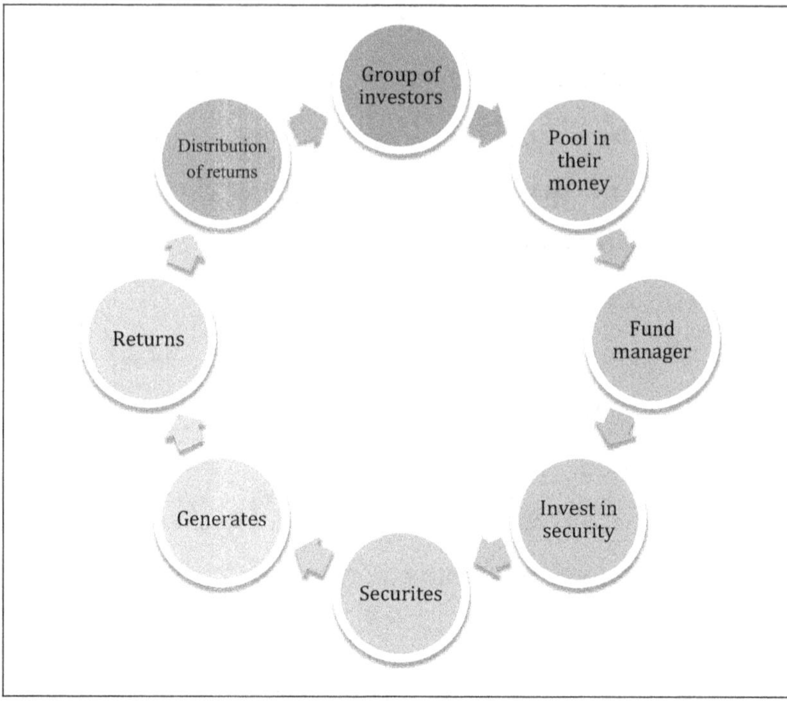

4.2.1 Types of mutual funds:

Each fund has a predetermined investment objective that tailors the fund's assets, regions of investments and investment strategies. At the fundamental level, mutual funds can be classified on three parameters:

A. On the basis of structure:

1. Open-ended mutual fund:

- Free entry-free exit
- Repurchasing facility
- Income generation
- Duration is not fix

2. Close-ended Mutual fund:

- For entry &exit time is fixed.
- No repurchasing facility.
- Capital appreciation
- Duration is fixed min. 3 year

B. On the basis of investment objective:

1. **Income fund**: - This fund provides a regular income
2. **Growth fund**: - Long run gain capital appreciation.
3. **Balanced fund**: - Regular income as well as capital appreciation.
4. **Taxation fund**: - It offers tax rebates to the investors.

Types of Mutual Fund (Figure-3)

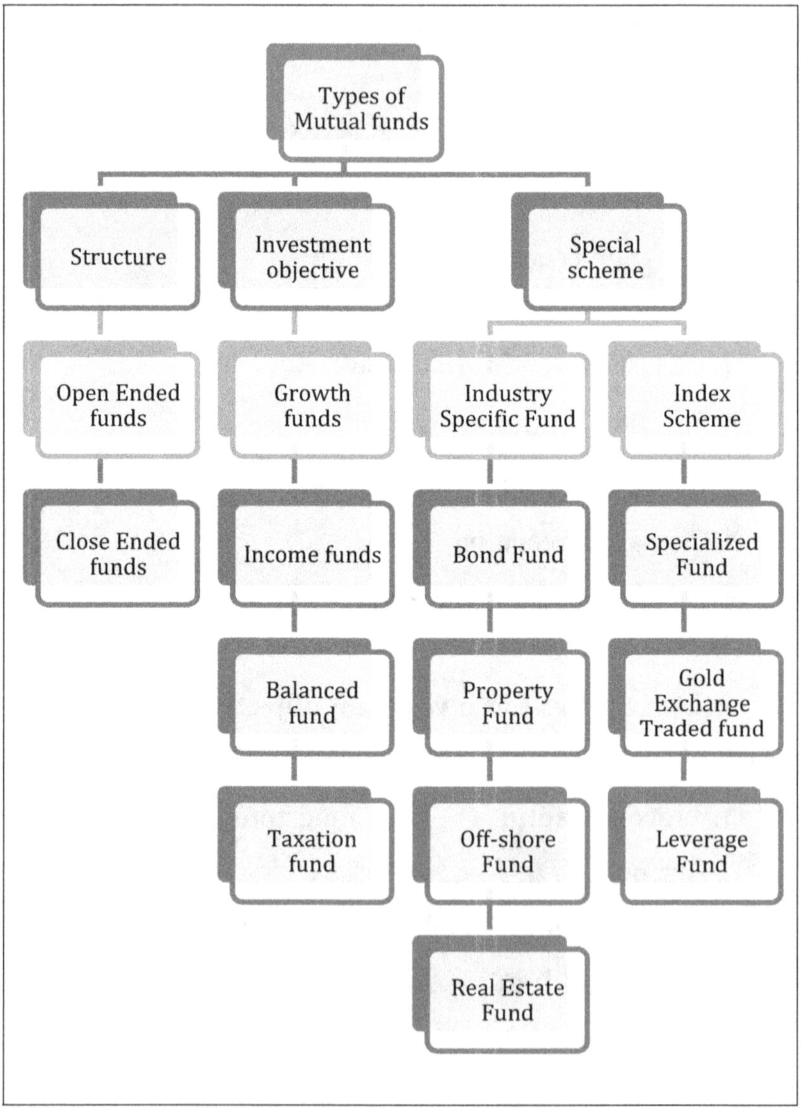

C. On the basis of special schemes

1. Industry Specific Fund:

- **Bond Fund:** This fund is also known as debt fund in this type of mutual fund the fund manager invests the money of investors in the bonds or in other debt instruments. Bond funds usually pay the higher returns.

- **Property Fund:** Investment in Commercial property like offices, factories, warehouses and retail spaces.

- **Off-shore Fund:** It is also known as International fund it is the mutual fund scheme which invest in the international market. These schemes invest in equities of a region or country.

- **Real Estate Fund:** In this fund the fund manager invests the money in securities of companies from the real estate sector.

2. Index Scheme:

Index fund is passive fund, so its expense ratio is lower than other funds. Index funds tracks the performance of the indices and the returns based on the performance of indices. In simple words the fund managers invest the money directly in indices (Sensex, Nifty). For e.g. HDFC Nifty funds, HDFC Sensex funds etc.

3. Specialized Fund:

These funds focus on the particular sector or industry to invest in. These funds offer good coverage to a market; they have much higher profit potential but it also carries the more risk because of the less diversification.

4. Gold Exchange Traded Fund:

It is a commodity based mutual fund that invests in assets like gold, these funds are traded like individual stocks on stock exchange.

5. **Leverage Fund:**

   Leverage funds are mutual funds using aggressive investment techniques like short selling and option trading, to gain more returns.

4.3 Debentures & Bonds:

Debentures and Bonds are instruments of acknowledgement of debt under the common seal of a company. Debentures and bonds are essentially long-term debt instruments having fixed rate of interest on them. After the specific time a company has to pay the full amount which is raised from the debenture holders.

❖ **Features: -**

- A debenture acknowledges a debt.
- It is in the form of certificates issued under the seal of the company. It usually shows the amount & date of repayment of the loan.
- It has a rate of interest & date of interest payment.
- Debentures are generally freely transferable by the debenture holder.
- Debenture holders have no rights to vote in the company's general meetings of shareholders.

4.3.1 Types of Debentures:

1. **Registered debentures:** Registered debentures are registered with the company. Debenture interest is paid only to that person whose name is registered in the register of the company.
2. **Bearer debentures**: Bearer debentures are not recorded in the register of a company. Bearer debentures are transferable. The holders of these debentures are eligible to get the interest.
3. **Secured debentures:** Secured debentures are secured by a charge on the company's asset. It gives the holders a right to recover principal amount with any unpaid interest out of the assets mortgaged by the company.
4. **Unsecured debentures:** These types of debenture holders don't have any charge on the company's assets; they have no claim on company's asset.
5. **Redeemable debentures:** Redeemable debentures are issued for a fixed period. On the expiry of the fixed period, the debentures holders are paid the principal amount.

6. **Non-Redeemable Debentures:** Non-redeemable debentures cannot be redeemed in a company's lifetime. Non-redeemable debentures are only paid back on company's liquidation.
7. **Convertible debentures:** Convertible debentures can be converted into shares of the company on completion of a pre-decided period. The terms and conditions of the conversion are announced at the time of issue of the debentures.
8. **Non-Convertible debentures:** Non-convertible debentures can't be converted into the shares of the company.

4.4 Government securities:

Government securities refer to the marketable debt instruments issued by the government or semi-government bodies. A government security is a claim on the government and totally secured financial instrument. These securities carry some tax advantages also.

❖ **Features:**

- Issued by the government because of this it's Fully safe and secured.
- Provides Tax benefits.

4.5 Money Market instruments:

Money market securities have very short-term maturity that is less than a year. Money market securities like treasury bills, commercial paper and certificates of deposit.

1. **Treasury Bills (T-Bills):**

   A treasury bill is a short-term money market instrument issued by RBI for the government for financing the temporary funding requirements. Treasury bills have tenor like 14 days, 91 days, 182 days and 364 days.

2. **Commercial paper (CP):**

   It represents short-term unsecured promissory notes issued by firms that enjoy a very much high credit-rating. Generally large firms with considerable financial strength are able to issue commercial paper.

3. **Certificate of deposits (CD):**

   A certificate of deposit (CD) represents a negotiable deposit with a commercial bank and they provide attractive interest rate. Certificate Deposits are freely transferable by approval and delivery after 15 days of the date of issue.

4.6 Derivatives:

Derivative is a product whose value is derived from the underlying asset in a contractual manner. The underlying asset can be equity, foreign exchange, commodity or any other asset. Derivative products are helpful for reducing the risk of price fluctuations.

4.6.1 Types of Derivatives:

1. **Forward:** It's a contract between buyer and seller of the underlying asset on a predetermined date, price and quantity.

❖ **Advantages:**

- Forwards are over-the-counter products.
- Forwards provide price protection.
- It offers a complete hedge.
- Forwards are tailor made and can be written for any amount and term.

❖ **Disadvantages:**

- Counterparty risk of defaulting on the contract is too high.
- Market of forward contracts is extremely unorganized.
- Difficult to find a counterparty to enter into a contract.

For E.g.

Mr Rahul is a farmer he has 500kg Apples,

Today's Market value of apples is 50Rs. Per Kg,

Appy's is a packaged juice making company, according to the market conditions the price of apples is fluctuating, after 2 months it can be Rs.40 or Rs.60 as well so Company and Mr Rahul decided to make a contract on today's date. According to that contract the company purchases the 500kg Apples from Mr Rahul after 2 months at Today's market value which is 50Rs. per kg. This contract is known as a Forward contract.

In this example of Mr Rahul is a seller, Appy's Company is a Buyer and Apples are the underlying asset.

2. **Futures:** Future derivatives are financial contracts that obligate the parties to transact an asset at a predetermined future date and price. The buyer must purchase or the seller must sell the underlying asset at the set price at the expiration date.

❖ **Advantages:**

- Easy pricing
- High liquidity
- Risk hedging.

❖ **Disadvantages:**

- No control over future events
- Price fluctuations
- The potential reduction in asset prices as the expiration date approaches.

3. **Options:** An option gives the right to buy or sell an underlying asset on or before a given date at a predetermined price. There are two types of options- call options and put options.

- **Call option:** A call option gives the **right to buy** a fixed number of shares of a particular stock, at a predetermined price on or before the expiration date.
- **Put option:** A put option gives the **right to sell** a fixed number of shares of a particular stock at a predetermined price on or before the expiry date.

- **For e.g.**

ABC Ltd. is trading in the market at 120/- a share. A contract (option) allowing the buyer of this contract to purchase 200 shares of ABC Ltd. stock at 120/- at any time in the next three months.

The seller will have agreed to deliver the 200 shares at this price on demand. For granting this option, the seller is paid a fee (premium) of 8 a share for each of the 200 shares covered by the contract.

If, within the next three months, a stock rises to 155/- a share, an option contract will be used by the buyer.

He will have purchased 200 shares of ABC Ltd. at 128 a share (120 contract price plus 8 per share premium) which is well below the 165 market price.

If the stock had declined to 110/- a share during the three-month period, the owner of the contract would do nothing. He will certainly not pay 120/- a share for stock worth only 110/-. The contract will expire. The seller of the contract will keep the 1,600/- premium. The buyer will be out of 1,600/-.

This example explains an options contract that gave the owner the right to purchase stock.

4. **SWAP:** A SWAP is a derivative contract in which two parties exchange the cash flows or liabilities from two different financial instruments. SWAPs don't trade on stock exchanges. SWAPs are OTC (Over The Counter) transactions between businesses or financial institutions that are customized to the needs of both parties.

❖ Types of SWAP derivative:

▪ Interest Rate SWAP:

An interest rate swap is an agreement in which one party exchange one set of interest rate payment for another rate over a time period. The most common arrangement is an exchange of fixed interest rate payment for another rate over a time period. The interest rates are calculated on notional values of principals.

▪ Currency Swaps:

The currency swap is an agreement between two parties to exchange (swap) payments or receipts in one currency for payment or receipts in other currency. Suppose if two entities are trading in currency, the rationale for currency swap between them lies in the fact that one borrower has a comparative advantage in borrowing in one currency, while the other borrower has an advantage in borrowing in another currency.

4.6.2 Participants in the derivatives market:

- **Hedgers:** Hedgers use futures or options markets to reduce or eliminate the risk associated with price of an asset.
- **Speculators:** Speculators use futures and options contracts to get extra leverage in betting on future movements in the price of an asset. They can increase both the potential gains and potential losses by usage of derivatives in a speculative venture.
- **Arbitrageurs:** Arbitrageurs are in business to take advantage of a discrepancy between prices in two different markets. If, for example, they see the futures price of an asset getting out of line with the cash price, they will take offsetting positions in the two markets to lock in a profit.

4.7 Commodities:

A commodity is a group of assets or goods that are important in daily life, like food, energy, metals. A commodity market involves buying, selling, or trading a raw product, such as oil, gold, or coffee.

The list of commodities traded in India as follows,

- **Bullion**: Gold, Silver
- **Base Metals**: Aluminium, Brass, Copper, Lead, Nickel, Zinc
- **Energy**: Crude oil, Natural gas
- **Agricultural commodities**: Black pepper, Cardamom, Castor seed, Cotton, Crude palm oil, Mentha oil, Palmolein, Rubber.

❖ **Advantages -**

- **Higher growth opportunities:** It provides a lot of opportunities to make quick income through commodity investment.

- **Provide security against inflation:** At the time of inflation the prices of goods and services increase, the value of commodities needed to produce these goods and services will automatically rise. By keeping some commodities in your investment portfolio, you can take advantage of market upswing.

- **Disadvantages -**

- **Highly volatile market:** Volatility makes commodities very risky for some traders. This one is a negative point of commodity trading.

- **Sometimes no income generation:** Just like other financial assets like stocks, bonds and Investment in commodities doesn't generate large income for the investor.

4.7.1 Mostly preferred commodities by investors

- **Crude oil**:

Crude oil is one of the mostly preferred commodities as there are several products that are produced as a result of refining crude oil such as petroleum, diesel, etc. The demand for crude oil is poised to increase with growing demand for automobiles. Top oil producing countries in the world are US, Saudi Arabia, Russia.

- **Gold**:

Gold is always considered as a haven. Whenever the US dollar prices fall, people start buying gold and when the price of dollar increases, gold prices fall. US dollar and gold prices share an inverse relationship.

There are six major commodity trading exchanges in India as listed below.

- Multi Commodity Exchange – MCX
- National Commodity and Derivatives Exchange – NCDEX
- National Multi Commodity Exchange – NMCE
- Indian Commodity Exchange – ICEX
- Ace Derivatives Exchange – ACE
- The Universal Commodity Exchange – UCX

Chapter-5

"Security Analysis"

5.1 Introduction:

Security Analysis refers to the process of estimating risk and return for securities. It includes analysis of various aspects of a security to determine it's value for investment decisions. Investments generally include assets or financial assets. Assets are tangible, material things like buildings, furniture, automobiles etc. Financial assets are pieces of paper representing an indirect claim to real assets in the form of Debt or Equity.

There are two main types of analysis as under,

5.2 Fundamental Analysis:

Fundamental analysis is useful for long term investment decision. In Fundamental Analysis Company's goodwill, it's performances, turnover, profitability & financial health has been checked &analysed with the help of ratio analysis. It shows the financial efficiency & financial position of a company.

Fundamental analysis is primarily concerned with determining the intrinsic value or the true value of a security. For determining the stocks intrinsic value, the details of all major factors like firm sales, expense, profit etc. is collected or normal prices earnings ratio.

After making this determination, the intrinsic value is compared with the current market price of stock. If the market price is greater than the intrinsic value the stock is said to be overvalued. If the market price is less than the intrinsic value, the stock is said to be undervalued.

Fundamental analysis includes:

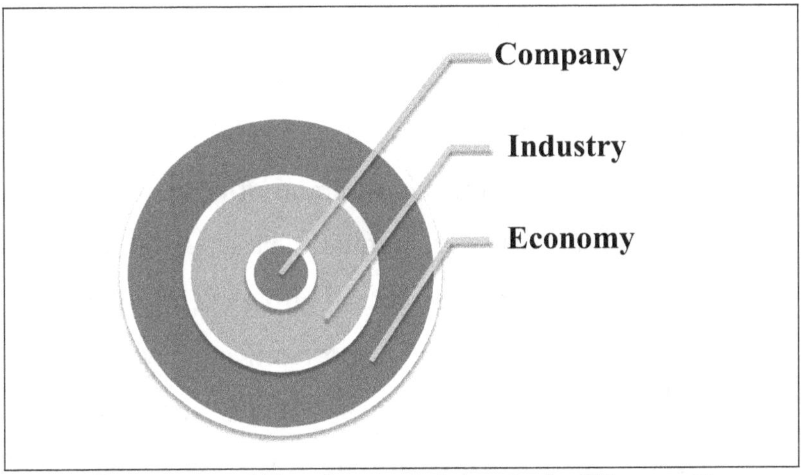

Structure of Fundamental Analysis (Figure-4)

- **Economic Analysis:**

Performance of a company is depending upon the overall economic environment of the country because demand for products and services of the company directly related to growth of the country's economy. If the country has an improving GDP growth rate, controlled inflation and increasing investment activity then chances for the valuation of securities can be liberal. The capital market is said to be in a bullish phase.

On the other hand, if the GDP growth rate decreases, inflation is out of control and investment activity is decreasing. The capital market enters a bearish phase and share values will decrease.

- **Industry Analysis:**

Industry analysis focuses on a particular industry rather than on the broader economy. An industry is a homogenous group of companies. That is, companies with similar characteristic can be divided into one industrial group. They face the similar problems and opportunities; they face the problems like technological changes, similar market competition, substitute products and services, consumer preferences etc. This problem depends on the industry life cycle.

The industry life cycle can be divided into three major stages-pioneering stage, expansion stage and stagnation stage. **The pioneering stage**s a starting phase of the industry. It is the stage when technological development takes places. The products have been newly introduced in the market. In the pioneering stage these products make extraordinary profits and thus attract competition.

In the **expansion stage** of the industry life cycle the demand for the products increases but at a lower price. There is less fluctuations in prices and production.

For these products' capital is easily available; Due to retention of profits, increase in internal growth.

At the **stagnation stage**, the growth rate slows down, there is no product innovation. External capital is hardly available at this stage. Even the internal capital is also not enough to fulfil the demand. This stage of the industry is most valuable during times of slowdown in national economy.

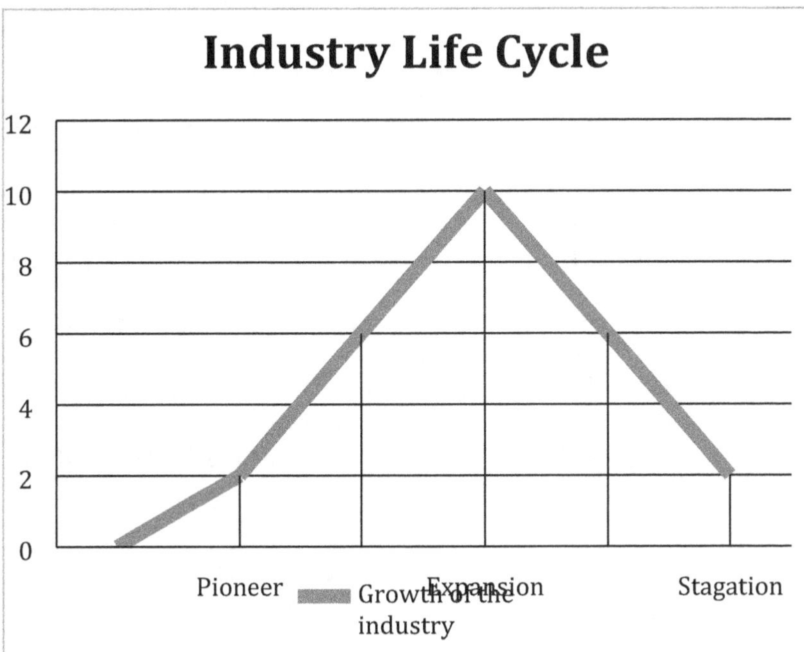

Industry Life Cycle (Figure-5)

- **Company Analysis:**

In the company analysis factors which affect the intrinsic value of stock has been analysed. There are two sides of company analysis quantitative analysis and the qualitative analysis.

The quantitative analysis includes the factors can be measured numerically like companies' assets, liabilities, cash flows, revenue. Some company's aspects which can't be measured in numerically Form. In the qualitative analysis includes the firm's overall business model, management staff, board of directors and the relationship between the shareholders and management.

5.2.1 Advantages of Fundamental Analysis:

- Fundamental analysis is good for long-term investment based on long-term trend.
- It helps to identify assets that represent a good value in long-term investment.
- It focuses on business and microeconomic factors of economy.
- It is systematic processes help us to determine the intrinsic value of a company's share with the help of statistical and analytical tools.
- It helps us in assessing the quality of management in terms of it's ability and honesty

.

5.2.2 Disadvantages of Fundamental Analysis:

- The biggest disadvantage of fundamental analysis is that its time consuming.
- Fundamental analysis is subjective, making use of so many assumptions and interpretations; all this requires lot of skills, knowledge and experience.

5.2.3 Tool of Fundamental Analysis:

Ratio Analysis is an important tool to analyse any business organization. It is a relationship between the two figures expressed arithmetically is called a ratio; which are connected with each other in some other manner.

Ratios are a very useful tool for grasping the true message of the financial statements and understanding them. Ratios may be worked out on the basis of figures contained in the financial statements. Ratios provide clues and symptoms of underlying conditions. They act as indicators of financial soundness, strength, position and status of a Company. There are various ratios used in the analysis they are as under,

1. **Price to Book Ratio (P/B):**

   This ratio, also known as the **price to equity ratio**, compares a stock's book value to its market value. The lower PB (less than 1) indicates that the stock is undervalued (i.e. a bad investment).
   Higher PB (More than 1) indicates that the stock is overvalued (i.e. it performed well)

Formula:

$$\textbf{PB Ratio} = \frac{Market\ value\ per\ share}{Book\ value\ per\ share}$$

2. **Earnings per Share (EPS):**

EPS shows How much of a company's profit is assigned to each share of stock. Earnings per share is calculated as a company's profit divided by the outstanding shares of it's common stock (equity shares).

Formula:

$$\textbf{EPS} = \frac{Net\ income - Preffered\ Dividend}{Outstanding\ Common\ Shares}$$

Example:

Name of the company: The bank of America

Net Income: 20, 00, 000

Preferred Dividends: 2, 00, 000

Outstanding Shares: 15, 000

Calculating EPS: $$\frac{20,00,000 - 2,00,000}{15000} = 120$$

3. **Dividend Yield:**

This is a ratio: yearly dividends compared to share price. It's expressed as a percentage. Divide dividends paid in a one-year period per share by the value of a share. 4% to 6% yield is considered as good yield.

Formula:

Dividend Yield = $$\frac{Dividend\ per\ share}{Share\ price}$$

Example:

	Company A	**Company B**
Share Price	**40**	**80**
Dividend per share	**2**	**2**
Dividend Yield Ratio	$\frac{2}{40} \times 100 = 5\%$	$\frac{2}{80} \times 100 = 2.5\%$

Interpretation:

As we can see in the above calculation it shows the company A's yield is 5% while company B's dividend yield is 2.5% so the investors choose the company A rather than B because it has a double dividend yield.

4. **Return on Equity:**

Divide the company's net income by shareholders' equity to find its return on equity. It shows how effectively management is using the company's asset to create profit. 15% to 20% ROE is generally considered good.

Formula:

$$\textbf{ROE} = \frac{Net\ Income}{\dfrac{Shareholder's\ Equity}{(Total\ Assets - Total\ Liabilities)}}$$

Example:

Company A is having annual income of 18, 00,000 and Shareholder's Equity is 120, 00,000

$$\textbf{ROE} = \frac{18{,}00{,}000}{120{,}00{,}000} \times 100$$

$$= \mathbf{15\%}$$

Interpretation:

According to the calculation the company's ROE is 15% which considered as good as per the standards so it concludes that the company's management is utilizing the resources and assets in good manner to create profit.

5. **Projected Earnings Growth (PEG):**

PEG predicts the one-year earnings growth rate of the stock. If the PEG Ratio is more than **1** then it means the stock is overvalued, if it's less than **1**then it means the stock is undervalued.

Formula:

$$\textbf{PEG} = \frac{Price\ to\ earning}{EPS\ Growth\ rate}$$

EPS Growth Rate =

$$\frac{EPS\ Current\ year - EPS\ Last\ year}{EPS\ Last\ year} \times 100$$

Example:

	ABC	XYZ
Price per share	**50**	**40**
EPS(2020)	**5**	**2**
EPS(2019)	**3**	**0.50**

EPS Growth rate	$\frac{5-3}{3} \times 100 = 66\%$	$\frac{2-0.50}{0.50} \times 100 = 300\%$
PEG	$\frac{10}{66}$ = **0.1515**	$\frac{20}{300}$ = **0.066**

Interpretation:

According above calculation the stock of XYZ .ltd is having the PE ratio 20%, Growth rate is 300% and PEG ratio is 0.07 it means the stock is undervalued with good growth rate so the XYZ .ltd is a good choice to invest as compared to ABC .ltd

6. **Price to Earnings Ratio (P/E):**

   This ratio compares the current sales price of a company's stock to it's per-share earnings. The ratio is used to for valuating companies and it shows the whether the price of shares is overvalued or undervalued.

Formula:

P/E= $\frac{\textit{Market price of the stock}}{\textit{EPS (Earning per share)}}$

7. **Price to Sales Ratio (P/S):**

The price to sales ratio values a company's stock price as compared with its revenues. From the investment perspective a Low PSR (1 or less) may indicate a good buy with a stock price is undervalued.

High PSR like 2 or 3 it shows the strong market price and strong company.

Formula:

$$\textbf{P/S Ratio} = \frac{Market\ value\ per\ share}{Sales\ per\ share}$$

Example:

Company A	2019	2020
Total sales	5000	6000

Outstanding shares	**1000**	**1000**
Sales Per shares	$\frac{5000}{1000} = 5$	$\frac{6000}{1000} = 6$
Market value per share	**5**	**5**
P/S Ratio	$\frac{5}{5} = 1$	$\frac{5}{6} = 0.83$

Interpretation:

As we can see the P/S ratio of Company A is decreased from 1 to 0.83 which is good sign. To find out the Company a stock is Overvalued or Undervalued we need to compare it with industry P/S ratio. Assume the industry ratio is 1; Then it can be concluded that company's stock is trading at a premium valuation in 2019 but is expected to see fall in valuation in the year 2020.

8. Dividend Pay-out Ratio:

This compares dividends paid out to the stockholders to the company's total net income. A High DPR means the company is reinvesting less money back into business. While paying out relatively more of it’s earnings in the form of dividends.

A Low DPR means that the company is reinvesting more money back into business for further expansions. A range of 35% to 55% is considered healthy and appropriate for a dividend investor’s point of view.

Formula:

$$\textbf{Dividend Pay-out Ratio} = \frac{Dividend\ per\ share}{Earning\ per\ share}$$

5.3 Technical Analysis:

Technical analysis refers to the study of market generated data like prices & volume to determine the future of prices movements. Technical analysis mainly helps to predict the short term price movements. It is important criteria for selecting the company to invest.

It also provides the base for decision-making in investment. For that matter a verity of tools was consider. This Technical analysis is helpful to general investor in many ways. It provides important & vital information regarding the current price position of the company. Technical analysis involves the use of various methods for charting, calculating & interpreting graph & chart to assess the performances & status of the price. It is the tool of financial analysis, which not only studies but also reflecting the numerical & graphical relationship between the important financial factors.

The focus of technical analysis is mainly on the internal market data, i.e. prices & volume data.

5.3.1 Advantages of Technical Analysis:

- It can be applied to virtually any trading instrument and in any timeframe.

- **Market news reflects the stock prices**:
  The stock price is a reflection of all fundamental news. It's used for price forecasting. This helps investors make informed investment decisions.

- **Trend identification**:
  The direction of the stock market trend is identified using technical analysis. The stock may be in an uptrend, a downtrend, or a sideways trend. The trend direction is useful when you're investing and trading in stock markets.

- **Entry and exit recommendations**:

Entry and exit strategy is recommended for short and long-term trading in technical analysis.

5.3.2 Disadvantages of technical analysis:

1. **Technical indicators' mixed signals:**

   One of the technical indicators will show a buy signal and another indicator will show a sell signal. This causes confusion in trading decisions.

2. **Accuracy:**

   Technical analysis is used to forecast stocks. All of the technical indicators give possible entry and exit points.

3. **Partial opinion:**

   One technical analyst's opinion may oppose another analyst's opinion for the same stock. The technical methods that are used to analyse stocks can vary from one analyst to another.

5.3.3 Tools of Technical Analysis:

Basically this analysis is done from the following four important points of view:

1. **Prices**: Whenever there is change in prices of securities, it is reflected in the changes in investor attitude and demand and supply of securities.

2. **Time**: The degree of movement in price is a function of time. The longer it takes for a reversal in trend, greater will be the price change that follows.

3. **Volume**: The strength of price changes is reflected in the volume of transactions that accompany the change. If an increase in price is accompanied by a small change in transactions, it implies that the change is not strong enough.

4. **Width**: The quality of price change is measured by determining whether a change in trend spreads across most sectors and industries or is concentrated in few securities only. Study of the width of the market indicates the extent to which price changes have taken place in the market in accordance with a certain overall trends.

There are various tools and techniques used to do technical analysis. To analyse these four factors there are various tools used in technical analysis we're going to see some of them as follows,

5. Trend Lines:

Trend lines are lines drawn on a price chart of an asset, just under or over the asset's local axis highs or lows, to indicate that price is following a particular direction.

These lines exist based on the natural placement of buy or sell orders by market participants, and the raising or lowering of stop loss levels, or where natural profit-taking may occur. A trend line typically is required to have multiple touches to be considered valid, and traders are recommended to watch for a break and close above or below trend lines, before taking any action. However, trend lines can also be used to help a trader make a decision even before the trend line has been breached and is no longer valid.

These trend lines also represent helpful guides for where a trader or investor may be interested in opening or exiting a position to maximize gain and minimize risk.

There are three basic kinds of trends,

- An Uptrend in where usually prices are increasing.

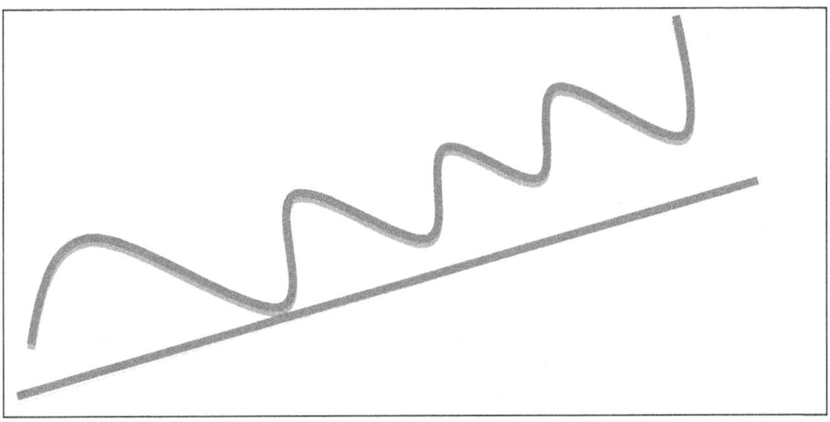

Uptrend (Figure-6)

- A Down trend where prices are usually decreasing.

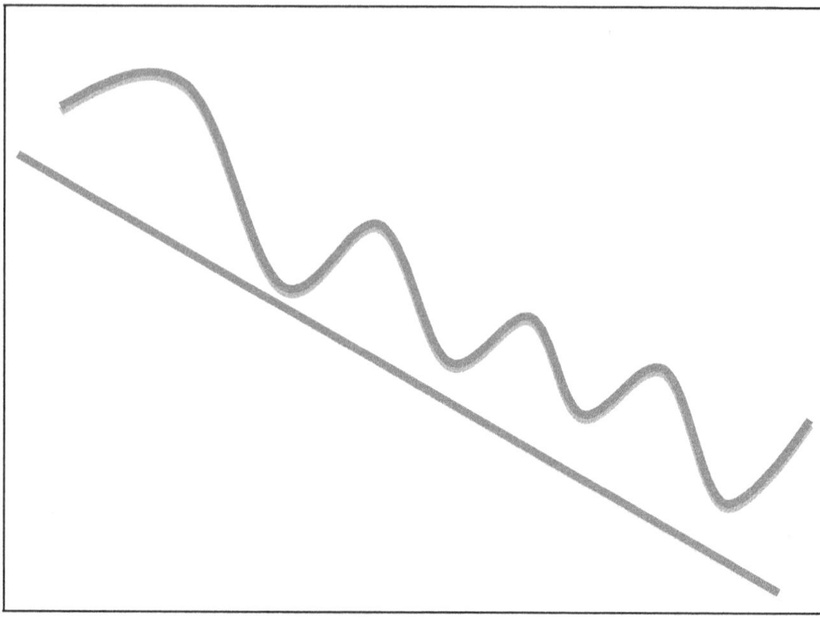

Down Trend (Figure-7)

- A trading ranges.

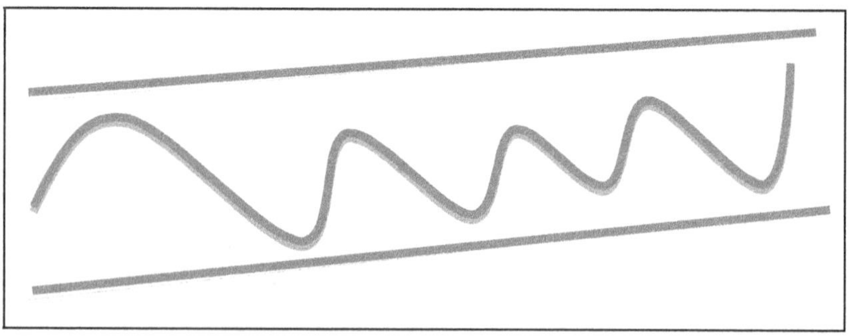

Trading Range (Figure-8)

6. Support and Resistance Levels:

Technical analysis use support and resistance levels to identify price points on a chart where the probabilities favour a pause or reversal of a prevailing trend. Support and resistance lines indicate likely ends of trends. Resistance occurs where an uptrend is expected to pause temporarily, due to a concentration of supply. Resistance level arises due to selling interest when prices have increased. Support is a price level where a downtrend can be expected to pause due to a concentration of demand or buying interest.

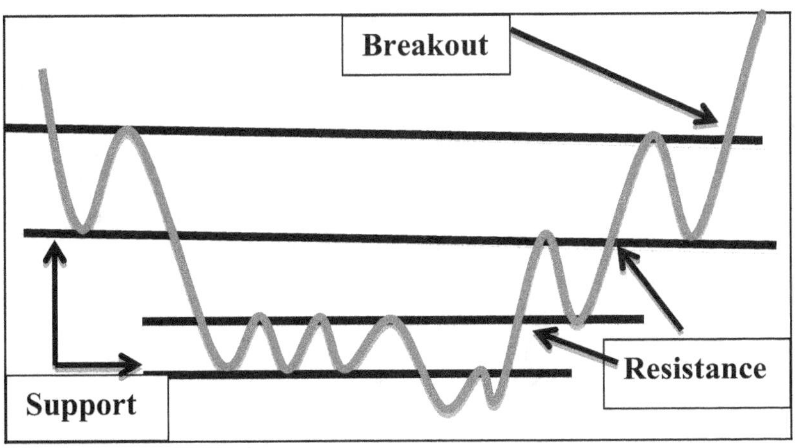

Support and Resistance Level (Figure-9)

7. Moving Averages

Moving averages are an indicator covered over price charts that represents the average price of an asset across a certain time period. Moving averages can be short- or long-term, across daily, weekly, or even longer timeframes.

Investors and traders usually use moving averages to find levels that may act as support or resistance and also to understand if a trend in an asset class is changing. A moving average simplifies price data by smoothing it out and creating one flowing line. This makes seeing the trend easier.

Moving Average (Figure-10)

(Source: www.investopedia.com)

8. Trading Volume

Trading volume is another extremely important tool for traders to use to determine interest in an asset. Trading volume is the total number of shares of a security that were traded during a given period of time. Trading volume is a technical indicator because it represents the overall activity of a security or a market. Essentially, trading volume can legitimize a security's price action, which can supports an investor in their decision to either buy or sell that security.

9. Candlesticks

Japanese candlesticks were introduced to assist technical analysts and traders in getting tipped off of upcoming price movements. Depending on how a candlestick opens, closes, and the price action within each candle can cause a candlestick to close in a particular shape or pattern. These shapes or patterns of candlesticks can also be used to predict future price movements.

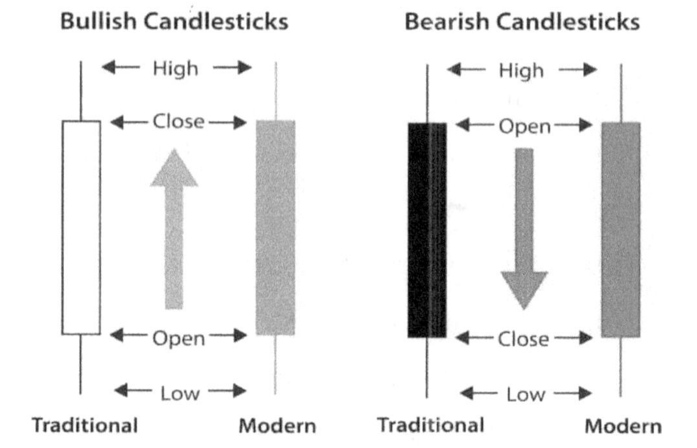

Candlestick Analysis (Figure-11)

10. Indicators

In addition to volume, other helpful indicators have been developed to add to a trader's store and offer even more changes to determine future price movements before they occur.

Commonly used indicators include the Stochastic Oscillator, Bollinger Bands, the Acceleration Deceleration indicator, and the MACD – the Moving Average Convergence Divergence indicator.

11. Fractals

Fractals are repeating patterns that play out on price charts, oftentimes on increasingly lower timeframes. Fractals also refer to a recurring pattern that occurs during larger more disordered price movements. Fractals are composed of five or more bars. The rules for identifying fractals are as follows:

A bearish turning point occurs when there is a pattern with the highest high in the middle and two lower highs on each side.

A bullish turning point occurs when there is a pattern with the lowest low in the middle and two higher lows on each side.

The fractals shown below are two examples of perfect patterns.

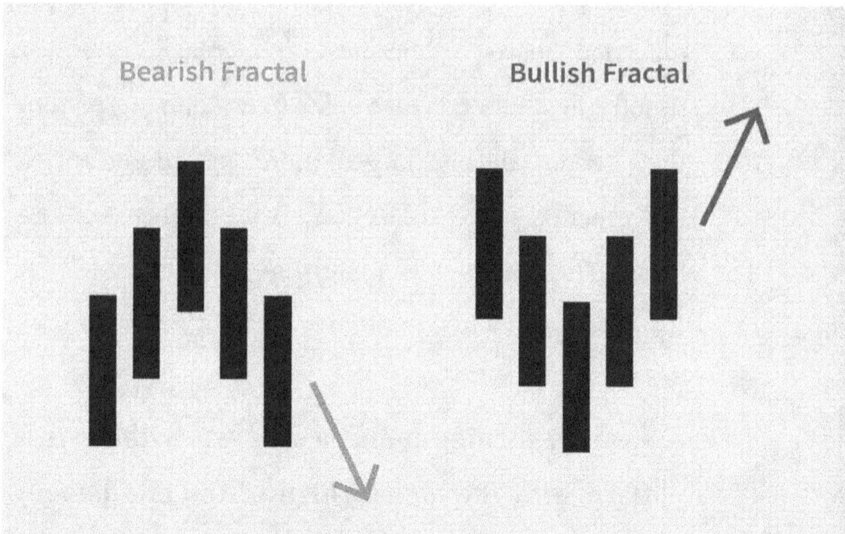

Fractals (Figure-12)

(Source: www.investopedia.com)

The technical analysis is the very much difficult analysis technique to understand and study. There are number of technical indicators, methods, statistical techniques, charts and different chart patterns have been used to analyse the securities.

Chapter-6

"Portfolio Management"

6.1 Introduction

6.1.1 Definition

6.1 Introduction

"Portfolio" means the total holdings of securities belonging to any person. Portfolio management is a decision - support system that helps investors to achieve the goal of investment. Portfolio Management is a process in which the investor invest his money in different types of financial assets rather than investing in one particular asset, because of this the risk of investment is divided in different types of financial assets if one of them is not performing well then other financial assets will help the investor to recover the loss. It helps to earn maximum return in minimum risk.

In other words, someone has given you their hard earned money and you need to help them to increase the capital in the best of different ways. This should be a way in which the risk return ratio is properly maintained considering the profits in mind and the time period of investments. Portfolio management refers to managing an individual's investments in the form of bonds, shares, cash, mutual funds etc. so that he earns the maximum profits within the specified time. A portfolio is built based on investor's income, investment budget and risk desired keeping the expected rate of return in mind.

6.1.1 Definition

- "Portfolio management is a systematic process of selecting the best way to invest money in such a way to earn maximum returns in minimum risk"

6.2 Why it is important?

Portfolio management plays very important role in respect of issuer and investor means companies and investors. After research portfolio manager decide which security or which other product is good or investible, accordingly he prepare strategies to invest. On the basis of the strategies he structures a portfolio.

According to research portfolio manager decide Weightage for the selected companies and distribute the share to that particular portfolio. It also involves market clearing process i.e. taking delivery of share and making payment for those shares.

Portfolio management helps to achieve the investment objective of the investors such as;

- **Security/Safety:** Portfolio management provides protection for investment against loss. To provide safety, a careful review of economic and industry trends is necessary. In other words, mistakes in portfolio are unavoidable and it requires broad diversification. Even investor wants that his basic amount of investment should remain safe.

- **Stability of Income:** Portfolio management provides stability in income because it works on planning more accurately and systematically to earn good returns.

- **Marketability:** This is important for providing flexibility to investment portfolio.
- **Capital Growth:** Capital appreciation is an important investment objective. Investors look for a growth stock which provides them a large capital

appreciation by way of rights, bonus and appreciation in the market price of a share. This can be achieved by reinvesting in growth securities.

- **Liquidity:** It is necessary for investor to take advantage of attractive opportunities upcoming in the market. It helps to maintain the liquidity of portfolio.

- **Diversification:** It is the basic objective of building a portfolio to reduce risk of loss of capital and to earn regular income by investing in various types of securities.

- **Tax Benefits:** By minimizing the tax burden, returns can be effectively improved; so the investors try to minimize their tax liabilities through the investments. The portfolio manager has to keep a list of such investment avenues which provides tax benefits as well as good returns.

6.3 Types of Portfolio Management:

- **Active Portfolio Management:** As the name proposes, in an active portfolio management service, the portfolio managers are actively involved in buying and selling of securities to ensure maximum profits to individuals.

- **Passive Portfolio Management:** In a passive portfolio management, the portfolio manager deals with a fixed portfolio designed to match the current market scenario.

- **Discretionary Portfolio management services:** In Discretionary portfolio management services, an individual allows a portfolio manager to take care of his financial needs on his behalf. The individual pay the fees to the portfolio manager in return he will take care of all his investment needs, paper work, documentation etc. In discretionary portfolio management, the portfolio manager has full rights to take decisions on behalf his client.

- **Non-Discretionary Portfolio management services:** In non-discretionary portfolio management services, the portfolio manager can only advise the client what is good and bad for him but the client reserves full right to take his own decisions.

6.4 Who is Portfolio manager?

An individual who understands the client's financial needs and designs a suitable investment plan as per his income and risk taking abilities is called a portfolio manager. A portfolio manager is one who takes an investment decisions on behalf of his client.

6.4.1 Role of Portfolio manager:

A portfolio manager is a person who makes investment decisions using money of his clients have placed under his control. They work with a team of financial analysts and researchers they are responsible for establishing an investment strategy, selecting suitable investment avenues.

Portfolio managers make decisions about investment mix and policy, matching investments to objectives, asset allocation for individuals and institutions, and balancing risk against performance. Some important key roles and responsibilities are as follows,

- Understand the clients risk taking abilityand needs by taking into account his liquidity, income, time horizon, expectations.

- Do the best asset allocation and choose strategy that meets the client's needs.

- Diversify the portfolio to reduce the unsystematic risk.

- Monitor the changing market scenario, expectations, client needs etc. and rebalance the portfolio as the clients requirement.

- Minimize the transaction cost by minimizing the taxes, trading turnover, and liquidity costs.

6.5 Process of Portfolio Management:

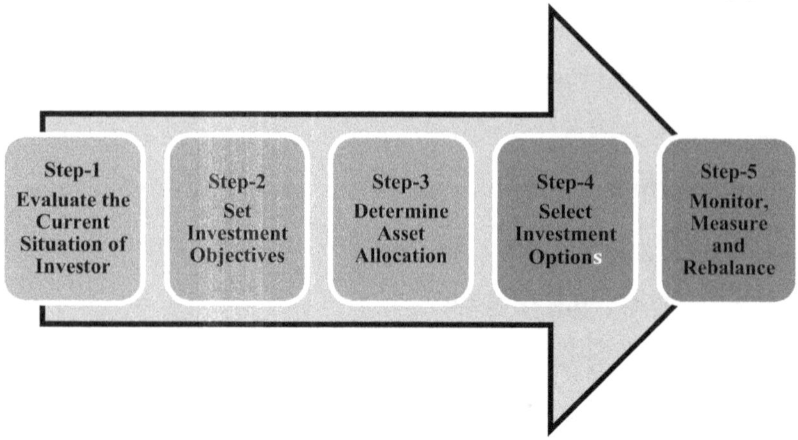

Process of Portfolio Management (Figure-13)

Step 1: Evaluate the Current Situation of Investor:

Before start Planning for the future requires a clear understanding of an investor's current situation about income, debt, investment budget, current assets, liabilities, cash flows and most importantly investment objectives. The objectives of investment must be clearly defined to make a strategy. This step needs to include a discussion about the investor's values, beliefs, and priorities; these all factors help to develop a best investment strategy.

Step 2: Set Investment Objectives:

Before setting the investment objective the risk taking ability of an investor must be defined. It helps to understand how much risk investor can take and how much volatility of market he can bear; it helps to formulate an investment objective. To evaluate the performance of portfolio we need to set the benchmarks to track the performance portfolio. Tracking the portfolio's performance against benchmarks allows smaller adjustments to be made as per the standards.

Step 3: Determine Asset Allocation:

In the financial market there are different types of financial instruments available in the market with different characteristics and risk-return percentage. By using the risk-return ratio of a investor can help to develop an asset allocation strategy with maximum diversification to reduce the risk. Selecting from various asset classes and investment options, the investor can allocate assets in a way that achieve the investment objective and expected returns. The asset allocation strategy is based on investor's current situation and goals.

Step 4: Select Investment Options:

Individual investment options are selected on the basis of asset allocation strategy. The selected investment type depends on the investor's preference for active or passive management.

Step 5: Monitor Measure and Rebalance:

After implementing a portfolio plan, the management process begins. This includes monitoring the investments and measuring the portfolio's performance on set benchmarks. It is necessary to report investment performance at regular intervals, quarterly, and to review the portfolio plan annually. Once a year, the investor's situation and goals get a review to determine if there have been any important changes made. If the performance is not well then the portfolio can be rebalanced by selling investments that have reached their targets, and buying new investment options that helps the portfolio to rebalance the performance.

When the investor is investing to achieve long term goals, the portfolio planning process will never stop. As per the changes occur, or as market or economic conditions, the portfolio planning process begins again.

6.6 Example of Portfolio Management:

Mr Ramesh has Rs.1, 00,000 to start investment in stock market but he didn't have enough knowledge about it; so he hires the portfolio manager to manage his portfolio. The Portfolio manager makes an investment strategy according to the client's risk-taking capacity and the expected returns.

So for example, the portfolio can include real estate, fixed deposits with banks, mutual funds, shares, and bonds. The principal amount of investment is divided into these five financial assets. So, depending on the security and the return from these avenues the division is done.

Investment option	Investment Amount	Risks	Returns
Real estate	20,000	Average	Average
Fix deposit	15,000	High	Average
Mutual fund	15,000	Average	Average
Shares	35,000	Low	High
Bonds	20,000	High	Low

On the other hand, the portfolio can be stock specific as well. So, the division is done across researched stocks in the markets.

Investment option	Investment Amount	Risks	Returns
HUL	15,000	High	Average
Infosys	15,000	High	Average
Reliance Industries	20,000	Average	Average
Navneet Education	30,000	Low	High
TCS	20,000	Low	High

Therefore, depending on the requirements of the investors, the fund manager takes suitable decisions and allocates the funds.

BIBLIOGRAPHY

- **Books:**

1) **Capital, Commodity And Money Market (Module 3)**
   The Institute Of Company Secretaries of India

2) **Financial Treasury And Forex Management (Module 2)**
   The Institute Of Company Secretaries of India

3) **Cost And Management Accounting (Module 1)**
   The Institute Of Company Secretaries of India

4) **Security Analysis & Investment Management**
   Directorate of Distance Education Guru Jambheshwar,
   University of Science and Technology, HISAR-125001

5) **Security Analysis and Portfolio Management (DCOM504/DMGT51)**
Lovely Professional University, Phagwara

6) **Security Analysis And Portfolio Management**
V. A. Avdhani

- **Websites:**

1) **www.investopedia.com**
2) **www.wikipedia.com**
3) **www.finnovationz.com**

INDEX

A

C

D

T

www.ingramcontent.com/pod-product-compliance
Lightning Source LLC
Chambersburg PA
CBHW062142160726
48282CB00027B/911
* 9 7 8 8 1 9 3 0 8 3 2 1 5 *